Wyoming. Laws Statutes

School Laws of the State of Wyoming in Force June 30, 1899

Wyoming. Laws Statutes

School Laws of the State of Wyoming in Force June 30, 1899

ISBN/EAN: 9783337225131

Printed in Europe, USA, Canada, Australia, Japan

Cover: Foto ©Suzi / pixelio.de

More available books at **www.hansebooks.com**

SCHOOL LAWS

. . . OF THE . . .

STATE OF WYOMING

In Force June 30, 1899.

Compiled by
THOS. T. TYNAN,
Superintendent of Public Instruction,
Cheyenne, Wyoming.

School Laws of the State of Wyoming.

DIVISION ONE.

TITLE III.   STATE OFFICERS.

CHAPTER 5.

SUPERINTENDENT OF PUBLIC INSTRUCTION.

GENERAL DUTIES.

Sec. 91. The duties of superintendent of public instruction shall be as follows: He shall file all papers, reports and public documents transmitted to him by the school officers of the several counties, each year, separately, and hold the same in readiness to be exhibited to the governor, or to any committees of either house of the legislature, and shall keep a fair record of all matter pertaining to the business of his office. He shall have a general supervision of all the district schools of the state, and shall see that the school system is, as early as practicable, put into uniform operation. He shall prepare and have printed suitable forms for all reports required by law, and shall transmit the same, with such instructions in reference to the course of studies as he may judge advisable, to the several officers entrusted with their management and care. He shall make all further rules and regulations that may be necessary to carry the law into full effect, according to its spirit and intent, which shall have the same force and effect as though contained herein.

[R. S. 1887, Sec. 3906.]

DISPOSITION OF DONATED BOOKS, MAPS AND SCHOOL APPARATUS.

Sec. 92. One copy of all books, maps, charts or school apparatus, which may be received by the superintendent of public instruction, from publishers, inventors or manufacturers, shall be placed by him in the public library of this state.

[R. S. 1887, Sec. 3907.]

DISTRIBUTION OF SCHOOL FUNDS.

Sec. 93. On or before the thirty-first day of March in every year, if there shall be any money to the credit of the income fund, for the use of public schools in the state treasury, including the rents of the unsold school lands, the state superintendent of public instruction shall distribute such income among the several counties of the state according to the number of children of school age in each, the same to be determined by reference to the last preceding annual reports furnished to the state superintendent of public instruction by the several county superintendents of schools. Such moneys so distributed shall be paid to the county treas-

3

urer of each county by the state treasurer, upon the requisition to that effect by the state superintendent of public instruction, which said requisition shall state the county entitled thereto, together with the amount, and the fund out of which it is to be paid; and the superintendent of public instruction shall at the same time notify each superintendent of schools that such distribution has been made; such requisition shall be accompanied by a warrant of the auditor upon the treasurer covering the amount of the requisition in each case, and the superintendent of public instruction shall file such requisition with the auditor and a copy of the same with the treasurer. Upon such distribution being made and said money being paid to the respective county treasurers, the county superintendent of schools in each county shall cause such money to be distributed among the several school districts in the county pro rata in the same manner and in the same proportion as the regular county school tax is required by law to be distributed. Provided, however, That any law with reference to the distribution of the county school tax which provides for a certain amount to be paid to each school district before the pro rata distribution of the balance is made shall not apply in the case of the distribution of said moneys; Provided further, That no apportionment from said state fund shall be made to any school district for a year in which a school has not been maintained therein for at least three months.

[See Div. 1, Tl. 6, Ch. 3, Art. VI.]   [S. L. 1895, Ch. 53, Sec. 1.]

BIENNIAL REPORTS OF STATE OFFICERS.

Sec. 180. Biennially, on or before the first day of November, immediately preceding the meeting of the legislature, each and every state officer (except those mentioned in the last preceding section), and each and every commission or board of a state institution, shall report in writing to the governor of the state, the condition of his department, or its institution, covering the period of two years preceding and up to and including the thirtieth day of September immediately preceding the filing of such report. The reports thus required to be filed shall be in triplicate, one copy to be filed in the office of the governor, one copy for the use of the senate, and one copy for the use of the house of representatives.

[S. L. 1890, Ch. 5, Sec. 1.]

DIVISION ONE.

TITLE X. COUNTY GOVERNMENT.

CHAPTER 16.

SUPERINTENDENT OF SCHOOLS.

OATH AND BOND—PROHIBITED FROM TEACHING.

Sec. 1190. There shall be in each organized county a superintendent of public schools, who shall, before entering upon the duties of his office, give bond to the state of Wyoming in the penal sum of five hundred dollars for the faithful performance of all duties required of him by law as such superintendent, to be approved by the board of county commissioners, and together with said certificate and oath, filed in the county clerk's office; Provided, That no person shall at the same time hold the position of county superintendent of public schools and teacher in any public school in his or her county. ‑

[R. S. 1887, Sec. 1898.]

SALARY.

Sec. 1191. County superintendents of schools shall receive the following annual salaries:

In counties of the first class, six hundred dollars; in counties of the second class, five hundred dollars; in counties of the third class, four hundred dollars; and in counties of the fourth class, three hundred dollars, together with his actual and necessary traveling expenses while engaged in the discharge of his official duties, the account for which expenses, before being allowed, shall be stated in separate items, accompanied by vouchers or receipts for all items amounting to five dollars or more, and otherwise made conformable to the law.

[S. L. 1895, Ch. 76, Secs. 6 and 14.]

DUTIES.

Sec. 1192. The duties of the county superintendent of schools shall be as follows: He shall on the first Monday of October in each year, transmit to the superintendent of public instruction a report, containing an abstract of the several particulars set forth in the reports of the district clerks, together with a statement of the financial affairs of his office, and such suggestions as he shall think proper, relative to the schools of his county; he shall distribute to the districts within his county such blank forms, circulars and other communications as may be transmitted to him for that purpose, by the superintendent of public instruction.

[S. L. 1895, Ch. 44, Sec. 1.]

Powder River Cattle Company vs. Board Commissioners, 3 Wyo. 597.
Baldwin vs. Wickman, 3 Wyo. 208.

5

APPORTIONMENT OF TAXES—DISTRICT TREASURER'S BOND.

Sec. 1193. On the first Monday of December, annually, he shall apportion the county school tax and all money in the county treasury, belonging to the school fund, in the following manner: Each school district in his county shall be apportioned the sum of one hundred and fifty dollars for the payment of teachers in such district, and all moneys remaining after such apportionment shall be apportioned to each district pro rata, in accordance with the number of pupils in attendance at the schools of said district, reported to him by the several district clerks; Provided always, That each, every and all poll taxes, levied and collected for school purposes, in each school district in this state, shall, when collected by the county treasurer, be paid over to the treasurer of the school district in which the persons respectively reside, who paid such poll tax, and the said poll taxes shall not be divided among the school districts of the county pro rata to the number of scholars in such school district, but the poll taxes so collected from the inhabitants of each school district shall be paid to the treasurer of the district in which they severally reside, for the support of the schools of such district; no district shall be entitled to the amount of one hundred and fifty dollars, for the payment of teachers, besides the pro rata apportionment as provided in this section, when there are less than eight scholars of school age in said district; he shall record a statement of such apportionment in his office, and he shall also notify the county treasurer of the same; he shall immediately draw an order on the county treasurer, in favor of the treasurer of each district for the amount of its proportion, and transmit the same to the treasurer of the district; Provided, Such district treasurer shall have given his official bond, which draft the county treasurer shall pay to the district treasurer on presentation of the draft properly endorsed.

[S. L. 1895, Ch. 44, Sec. 1.]

Powder River Cattle Co. vs. Board Commissioners, 3 Wyo. 597.
Baldwin vs. Wickman, 3 Wyo. 208.

SUPPLEMENTAL APPORTIONMENT.

Sec. 1194. Should no apportionment of the school funds be made on the first Monday in December, as required in this chapter, he may make an apportionment as soon thereafter as practicable, in the same manner as hereinbefore provided. He may also make a supplementary apportionment of the money in the county school fund at any time after the first Monday in December, prior to the first of the following June, and such supplementary apportionment shall be pro rata, according to the number of pupils in attendance in any and all schools in each district, as reported to him by the several district clerks in their last annual reports.

[S. L. 1895, Ch. 44, Sec. 1.]

Powder River Cattle Co. vs. Board Commissioners, 3 Wyo. 597.
Baldwin vs. Wickman, 3 Wyo. 208.

BOUNDARIES OF DISTRICTS WHEN CHANGED—NUMBER.

Sec. 1195. He shall divide the county into school districts, and may alter and change the boundaries of districts thus formed, from time to time as the convenience of the inhabitants of the aforesaid district may require, and shall proceed to make such change at any time, when petitioned by two-thirds of the legal voters of any district: Provided, That the number of districts in any county whose population is less than ten thousand, shall not exceed twenty-five; and in case the number of districts in any county exceeds the proportion above stated, it shall be the duty of the superintendent of such county, immediately to re-district

6

such county in accordance herewith. And the county superintendent of schools shall abolish or join in a contiguous district, any school district in which no school has been maintained for twelve consecutive months, and all funds to the credit of such district so abolished or joined to another district, shall be returned to, and become a part of the general school fund of the county: Provided, That nothing in this chapter shall be so construed as to prevent the county superintendent of schools from joining any school district (having less than eight pupils) to any other school district lying contiguous thereto, if, in the judgment of said superintendent, it will be for the benefit of the public schools, to so join such districts.

[S. L. 1895, Ch. 44, Sec. 1.]

Powder River Cattle Co. vs. Board Commissioners, 3 Wyo. 597.
Baldwin vs. Wickman, 3 Wyo. 208.

EXAMINATION OF TEACHERS—VISITS.

Sec. 1196. He shall examine every person offering himself or herself as a teacher of public schools under the provisions of section six hundred and thirty-one, and if in his opinion such person is qualified to teach a public school, shall give him or her a certificate as provided for in sections six hundred and twenty-seven and six hundred and twenty-eight, authorizing him or her to teach a public school in his county. He shall have the general superintendence of the schools of his county, and shall visit each school at least once each term, and shall have power to dismiss all teachers he may find to be incompetent.

[S. L. 1895, Ch. 44, Sec. 1.]

Powder River Cattle Co. vs. Board Commissioners, 3 Wyo. 597.
Baldwin vs. Wickman, 3 Wyo. 208.

FAILURE TO MAKE REPORT—PENALTY.

Sec. 1197. Should he fail to make his reports, as required in this chapter, he shall forfeit the sum of one hundred dollars, and suit shall be brought on his official bond for the collection of the same, with damages, by the prosecuting attorney.

[R. S. 1887, Sec. 3915.]

SUPERVISORY AND APPELLATE AUTHORITY.

Sec. 1198. He shall see that the annual reports of the clerks of the several school districts in his county are made correctly and in due time, and shall hear and determine all appeals from the decision of the district boards.

[R. S. 1887, Sec. 3917.]

COUNTY TEACHERS' INSTITUTE.

Sec. 1199. The county superintendent of public schools shall hold annually, at some convenient place, a county teachers' institute for the instruction and advancement of teachers. Said institute shall continue not less than four days nor more than five days. The county superintendent shall preside at all meetings, and determine the time and place for holding such institute. It shall be the duty of all teachers actually engaged in teaching in such county to attend such institute unless they shall have a written excuse, signed by the county superintendent. It shall be the duty of each district board to pay all teachers who attend such institute, the same salary per day they would have paid had the same amount of time been spent in teaching. It shall be the duty of the county board of commissioners in each county, to appropriate annually the sum of one hundred dollars for the payment of such instructors or lecturers as the county superintendent may employ to assist him in holding the county institute.

[S. L. 1888, Ch. 72, Sub. Div. 4, Sec. 1.]

DIVISION ONE.

TITLE VI. EDUCATIONAL INSTITUTIONS.

CHAPTER 1. THE UNIVERSITY OF WYOMING.
CHAPTER 2. THE WYOMING AGRICULTURAL COLLEGE.
CHAPTER 3. PUBLIC SCHOOLS.

CHAPTER 1.

THE UNIVERSITY OF WYOMING.

ESTABLISHMENT.

Sec. 485. There is established in this state, at the city of Laramie, an institution of learning under the name and style of "The University of Wyoming."

[S. L. 1890-91, Ch. 75, Sec. 1.]

OBJECT OF.

Sec. 486. The objects of such university shall be to provide an efficient means of imparting to young men and young women, without regard to color, on equal terms, a liberal education, together with a thorough knowledge of the various branches connected with the scientific, industrial and professional pursuits. To this end it shall embrace colleges or departments of letters, of science, and of the arts, together with such professional or other departments as in course of time may be connected therewith. The department of letters shall embrace a liberal course of instruction in language, literature and philosophy, together with such courses or parts of courses in the college or department of science as are deemed necessary.

[S. L. 1890-91, Ch. 75, Sec. 2.]

DEPARTMENTS.

Sec. 487. The college, or department of science, shall embrace courses of instruction in the mathematical, physical and natural sciences, together with such courses in language, literature and philosophy as shall constitute a liberal education. The college or department of the arts. shall embrace courses of instruction in the practical and fine arts; especially in the applications of science to the arts of mining and metallurgy, mechanics, engineering, architecture, agriculture and commerce, together with instruction in military tactics, and in such branches in the department of letters, as are necessary to a proper fitness of students for their chosen pursuits, and as soon as the income of the university will allow, in such order as the wants of the public shall seem to require, the said courses in the sciences and their practical applications shall be expanded into full and distinct schools or departments.

[S. L. 1890-91, Ch. 75, Sec. 2.]

BOARD OF TRUSTEES.

Sec. 488. The government of the university shall vest in a board of nine trustees to be appointed by the governor, three, and only three, of whom shall at all times be residents of the county of Albany, together with the president of the university and the state superintendent of public instruction, as members ex-officio as such having the right to speak, but not to vote.

[S. L. 1890-91, Ch. 75, Sec. 3.]

APPOINTMENT—TERM OF OFFICE.

Sec. 489. The term of office of the trustees appointed shall be six years. During each session of the legislature, the governor shall nominate, and by and with the advice and consent of the senate, appoint successors to the three trustees whose term of office shall have expired, or will expire before the next session of the legislature. Any vacancy in the board of trustees caused by death, resignation, removal from the state or otherwise, shall be filled by appointment to be made by the governor, which appointment shall continue until the next session of the legislature, and no longer, but no member of the faculty, while holding that position, shall ever be appointed a trustee.

[S. L. 1890-91, Ch. 75, Sec. 4.]

POWERS OF THE BOARD OF TRUSTEES.

Sec. 490. The board of trustees and their successors in office shall constitute a body corporate by the name of "The Trustees of the University of Wyoming." They shall possess all the powers necessary or convenient to accomplish the objects and perform the duties prescribed by law, and shall have the custody of the books, records, buildings and all other property of the university. The board shall have power to elect a president, secretary and treasurer, who shall perform such duties as are prescribed in the by-laws of the board. The treasurer shall execute such bond, with approved sureties in double the sum likely to come into his hands, for the faithful discharge of his duties as the board shall require. The term of office of said officers, their duties severally, and the times for holding meetings, shall be fixed in the by-laws of the board. A majority of the board shall constitute a quorum for the transaction of business, but a less number may adjourn from time to time, and all routine business may be entrusted to an executive committee of three members, subject to such conditions as the by-laws of the board shall prescribe. The actual and necessary traveling expenses of non-resident members in attending the annual meeting of the board may be audited by the auditing committee thereof, and paid by warrant on the treasurer out of the general fund of the university.

[S. L. 1890-91, Ch. 75, Sec. 5.]

BOARD TO PRESCRIBE GOVERNMENT.

Sec. 491. The board of trustees shall prescribe rules for the government of the university in all its branches, elect the requisite officers, professors, instructors and employes, any of whom may be removed for cause, as well as fix the salary and term of office of each, prescribe the studies to be pursued and the text-books to be used, and determine the qualifications of applicants for admission to the various courses of study; but no instruction either sectarian in religion or partisan in politics, shall ever be allowed in any department of the university, and no sectarian or partisan test shall ever be exercised or allowed in the appointment of trustees, or in the election or removal of professors, teachers or other officers of the university, or in the admission of students thereto, or for any purpose whatsoever. The board of trustees shall also have power to confer such degrees and grant such diplomas as are usual in universities, or as they shall deem appropriate; through by-laws, to confer upon the faculty the power to suspend or expel students for causes therein prescribed; to possess and use for the benefit of the institution, all property of the university; to hold, manage, lease, or dispose of, according to law, any real or personal estate, as shall be conducive to the welfare of the institution; to expend the income placed under their control, from whatever source derived, and finally to exercise any and all other functions properly belonging to such a board and necessary to the prosperity of the university in all of its departments.

[S. L. 1890-91, Ch. 75, Sec. 6.]

REPORT OF TRUSTEES.

Sec. 492. At the close of each scholastic year, (June 30th,) the trustees of the University of Wyoming, through their president, shall make a report in detail to the governor, exhibiting the progress, condition and wants of the university, and of each school or department thereof; the course of study in each, the number of professors and students, together with the nature, costs and results of important investigations, and such other information as they deem important, or as may be required by any law of this state, or of the United States. Accompanying such report, and as a part thereof, the secretary and treasurer of the board of trustees shall unite in an itemized report showing the amount of receipts and disbursements for the year, as had and made by said board, showing the appropriation resolution for that year, showing clearly the purposes for which the same have been expended, and the amount thereof expended upon each school or department of work, including the experiment station. Such reports are to be printed and not less than one hundred copies thereof filed with the secretary of state for distribution among the members of the legislature and other public officers.

[S. L. 1899, Ch. 61, Secs. 1 and 2.]

THE FACULTY AND ITS POWER.

Sec. 493. The president and professors of the university shall be styled "the faculty," and shall have power, as such body, to enforce the rules and regulations adopted by the trustees for the government of students, to reward and censure students as they may deserve, and generally to exercise such discipline, in harmony with the said regulations, as shall be necessary for the good order of the institution; to present to the trustees for degrees and honors such students as are entitled thereto, and in testimony thereof, when ordered by the board, suitable diplomas, certificates or other testimonials under seal of the university, and the signatures of the faculty. When, in course of time, distinct colleges or departments of the university are duly organized and in active operation, the immediate government of such departments shall, in like manner, be entrusted to their respective faculties.

[S. L. 1890-91, Ch. 75, Sec. 8.]

DUTY AND POWER OF PRESIDENT.

Sec. 494. The president of the university shall be president of the several faculties and the executive head of all the departments. As such, subject to the board of trustees, he shall have authority to give general direction to the instruction and investigations of the several schools and departments, and, so long as the interests of the institution require it, he may be charged with the duties of one of the professorships.

[S. L. 1890-91, Ch. 75, Sec. 9.]

SECRETARY SHALL TAKE OATH OF OFFICE.

Sec. 495. The secretary of the board of trustees, of the University of Wyoming, shall be required before entering upon the duties of said office, to take the oath of office provided for elective officers under the constitution of this state.

[S. L. 1897, Ch. 24, Sec. 1.]

SECRETARY MAY ADMINISTER OATHS.

Sec. 496. The secretary of the board of trustees of the University of Wyoming, is hereby authorized to administer oaths and affirmations to any person or persons, in connection with the business of the said University of the State of Wyoming.

[S. L. 1897, Ch. 24, Sec. 2.]

TUITION.

Sec. 497. To the end that none of the youth of the state who crave the benefits of higher education may be denied, and that all may be encouraged to avail themselves of the advantages offered by the university, tuition shall be as nearly free as possible, and it shall be wholly free to such students from each county as are selected and appointed by the board of county commissioners therein.

[S. L. 1890-91, Ch. 75, Sec. 10.]

DIPLOMA.

Sec. 498. After any student has been graduated from either of the chief departments of the university, and received the degree of bachelor of arts, of letters, of philosophy, or of science, and has had a subsequent experience as a successful teacher of a public school in Wyoming for a period of one school year, the state superintendent of public instruction shall have authority to countersign the diploma of such teacher after such examination as to moral character, learning and ability to teach as to the said superintendent may seem proper; and such graduate so tested shall, after his diploma has been so countersigned by the state superintendent, as aforesaid, be deemed qualified to teach any of the public schools of this state, and the diploma so countersigned shall be his certificate of such qualification until annulled by the state superintendent of public instruction.

[S. L. 1890-91, Ch. 75, Sec. 11.]

ACCEPTANCE OF CONGRESSIONAL APPROPRIATION.

Sec. 499. The University of Wyoming having been designated by the secretary of the interior as the proper institution to receive and expend the moneys appropriated by an act of congress, approved August thirtieth, eighteen hundred and ninety, entitled, "An Act to apply a portion of the proceeds of the public lands to the more complete endowment and support of the colleges for the benefit of agriculture and the mechanic arts, established under the provisions of an act of congress, approved July second, eighteen hundred and sixty-two," until such time as there may be an agricultural college established in this state, separate and apart from said University of Wyoming, assent is hereby given to all the terms and conditions of the said act of congress and the grants of money authorized and made by said act are hereby assented to and accepted by the state of Wyoming. The treasurer of the state of Wyoming is hereby designated as the proper officer to accept and receive said moneys so granted by said act of congress, and to disburse the same in accordance with the provisions of section two, of the said act of congress.

[S. L. 1890-91, Ch. 74, Secs. 1 and 2.]

EXPERIMENT STATIONS—APPROPRIATION.

Sec. 500. The University of Wyoming having been designated by the secretary of the interior as the proper institution to receive and expend the moneys appropriated by an act of congress approved August thirtieth, eighteen hundred and ninety, entitled "An act to apply a portion of the proceeds of the public lands to the more complete endowment and support of colleges for the benefit of agriculture and the mechanic arts, established under the provisions of an act of congress approved July second, eighteen hundred and sixty-two," until such time as there may be an agricultural college established in this state, separate and apart from the said University of Wyoming, assent is hereby given to all the terms and conditions of said act of congress, and grants of money authorized and made by said act, by the act of March second, eighteen hundred and eighty-seven, relative to the establishment of agricultural experiment stations, or any other act for like purposes, are hereby assented to and accepted by the state of Wyoming. Except where other designation is made by congress, all moneys granted or donated by congress in aid of scientific instruction or experimentation, and set apart by the legislature for such use by the University of Wyoming, shall be accepted and received by the state treasurer, and by him placed at the disposal of the board of trustees of the said university by transfer to the treasurer of said board, for disbursement in accordance with the provisions of the act or acts of congress aforesaid.

[S. L. 1890-91, Ch. 75, Sec. 13.]

LEGISLATURE SHALL MAKE APPROPRIATION.

Sec. 501. There shall be appropriations made by the legislature of the moneys intended for the support and maintenance of the University of Wyoming, and such appropriations shall specify as nearly and accurately as the same can be done, the specific purposes for which such moneys are intended and may be used. Such appropriations shall apply to and include all moneys received by the university from the United States for the endowment and support of colleges for the benefit of agriculture and mechanic arts; but moneys so received from the United States shall be appropriated, applied and used solely for the purpose specified in the acts of congress regulating the same. No expenditure shall be made in excess of such appropriation, and no moneys so appropriated shall be used for any purpose other than that for which they are appropriated.

[S. L. 1895, Ch. 110, Sec. 1.]

APPROPRIATION FOR EXPERIMENT STATIONS—HOW USED.

Sec. 502. The moneys received under an act of congress, approved March 2, 1887, entitled, "An Act to establish agricultural experiment stations in connection with the colleges established in the several states under the provisions of an act approved July 2, 1862, and of the acts supplementary thereto," shall be appropriated, used and expended pursuant to the provisions of this chapter, and not otherwise.

[S. L. 1895, Ch. 109, Sec. 1.]

APPROPRIATION—HOW EXPENDED.

Sec. 503. The trustees of the university or college at Laramie, Wyoming, in connection with which such experimental station is established shall annually, by resolution, specifically appropriate and designate the uses to which such money shall be applied and the purposes for which the same shall be expended. Such uses and purposes at all times to be within the use and purpose for which such money is donated under the acts of congress regulating the same, and no part of such money shall be used or expended in any manner or for any purpose not covered by such appropriation, and no indebtedness shall be contracted or expenditure made in excess of such appropriation.

[S. L. 1895, Ch. 109, Sec. 2.]

CHAPTER 2.

THE WYOMING AGRICULTURAL COLLEGE.

ESTABLISHMENT OF AN AGRICULTURAL COLLEGE.

Sec. 504. There shall be established in this state "The Wyoming Agricultural College," which shall be located by vote of the people, and which shall be a state public educational institution.

[S. L. 1890-91, Ch. 92, Sec. 1.]

(Under the provisions of sections 18 to 24 of chapter 92, laws of 1890-91, said college was located by vote of the people, in 1892, at Lander, Fremont county.)

OBJECTS.

Sec. 505. The objects of said agricultural college shall be to provide an efficient means of imparting to young men and young women, without regard to color, on equal terms, a liberal education and a thorough knowledge of such arts and sciences as will aid in the prosecution of agricultural pursuits with their varied applications.

[S. L. 1890-91, Ch. 92, Sec. 2.]

GOVERNMENT TRUSTEES.

Sec. 506. The government of said agricultural college shall be vested in a board of five trustees, who shall be appointed by the governor, by and with the advice and consent of the senate.

[S. L. 1890-91, Ch. 92, Sec. 3.]

TERM OF OFFICE—APPOINTMENT.

Sec. 507. The term of office of such trustees shall be four years, and during each session of the legislature the governor shall nominate and by and with the advice and consent of the senate, appoint successors to such of said trustees whose terms of office shall have expired or will expire during such session of the legislature.

[S. L. 1890-91, Ch. 92, Secs. 4 and 5.]

VACANCY—HOW FILLED.

Sec. 508. Any vacancy in the said board of trustees caused by death, resignation, removal from the state or otherwise, shall be filled by appointment to be made by the governor, which appointment shall continue until the next session of the legislature and no longer.

[S. L. 1890-91, Ch. 92, Sec. 6.]

QUORUM AND MEETINGS.

Sec. 509. A majority of the said board of trustees shall constitute a quorum for the transaction of business, and the said board shall hold regular meetings at the seat of the said agricultural college on the first day of the months of January, April, July and October of each year.

[S. L. 1890-91, Ch. 92, Sec. 7.]

POWER OF THE BOARD.

Sec. 510. The said board of trustees shall have power:

1. To elect one of its members president of said board.

2. To appoint a secretary and treasurer from among the members of such board and such other officers as it may deem necessary for the good order and government of the said agricultural college, and to prescribe the duties and fix the compensation of all such officers.

13

3. To provide by resolution or otherwise for special meetings of such board.

4. To procure by purchase, donation or otherwise, in the name of the state of Wyoming, within or near the limits of the city, town or village chosen as the seat of said agricultural college, a suitable site upon which to erect suitable, convenient and proper buildings for said agricultural college, and to superintend the erection of such buildings; Provided, That said trustees shall not purchase any site or contract for the erection of any building until the funds shall be in their hands with which to pay for the same.

5. To possess and use for the benefit of the said agricultural college, the buildings and sites that may be provided therefor.

6. To take and hold for the use and benefit of the said agricultural college any real or personal estate, and to dispose of the same in such manner as they may deem most conducive to the interests of said agricultural college.

7. To expend any and all income that may be placed under the control of such board, by donations or by law or otherwise, in such manner as shall best promote the interests and prosperity of the said institution.

8. To elect a president, such professors, tutors and other officers of the faculty of the said institution, as they may deem necessary, who shall hold their offices during the pleasure of such trustees.

9. To prescribe the duties, salaries and emoluments of such professors, tutors and officers.

10. To prescribe the course of study and discipline to be observed in said institution and the price of tuition therein.

11. To make all by-laws and rules necessary and proper to carry into effect the powers herein conferred.

[S. L. 1890-91, Ch. 92, Sec. 8.]

THE FACULTY AND THEIR POWERS.

Sec. 511. The president, professors and tutors of said agricultural college, shall be styled the faculty thereof, and as such shall have power:

1. To enforce the rules and regulations adopted by the trustees of said institution for the government of the students thereof.

2. To reprove and censure students as they may deserve, and to suspend those who continue refractory until a determination of the board of trustees can be had thereof.

3. To grant and confer, by and with the consent and approval of the trustees, such literary honors and degrees as are usually granted and conferred in institutions of the same class in the United States, and in testimony thereof to give suitable diplomas under the seal of the state and signatures of the faculty.

[S. L. 1890-91, Ch. 92, Sec. 9.]

MEMBER OF FACULTY CANNOT BE TRUSTEE.

Sec. 512. No member of the faculty of the said agricultural college, shall, while acting in that capacity, be a trustee.

[S. L. 1890-91, Ch. 92, Sec. 10.]

NO RELIGIOUS TEST.

Sec. 513. No religious qualification or test shall be required of any student, trustee, president, professor, tutor or officer of said institution, or as a condition for admission to any privilege in the same, and no sectarian tenets or principles shall be taught, instructed or inculcated at said institution, by any president, professor or tutor therein.

[S. L. 1890-91, Ch. 92, Sec. 11.]

WHO TO BE ADMITTED FREE OF CHARGE.

Sec. 514. The trustees of said institution shall provide for the tui-

14

tion, free of charge, of such students from each county as may be selected and appointed by the board of county commissioners of such county.

[S. L. 1890-91, Ch. 92, Sec. 12.]

DONATIONS—MANAGEMENT OF.

Sec. 515. In the management and application of any property, real or personal, granted, devised or bequeathed to the use of said agricultural college, or the proceeds thereof, the trustees shall conform to the will and directions of the donor thereof, if any such directions shall have been connected with such grant, devise bequest or donation.

[S. L. 1890-91, Ch. 92, Sec. 13.]

TREASURER TO GIVE BOND.

Sec. 516. The trustees of said institution shall require their treasurer to give a bond with sureties to be approved by them, in double the sum likely to come into his hands.

[S. L. 1890-91, Ch. 92, Sec. 14.]

DUTY OF SECRETARY.

Sec. 517. The secretary of said board of trustees shall keep a true record of the proceedings of the board and shall make and certify copies thereof. He shall also keep an account of the students in the institution, according to their classes, showing their respective ages and places of residence.

[S. L. 1890-91, Ch. 92, Sec. 15.]

DUTY OF TREASURER.

Sec. 518. The treasurer of said board shall keep full, true and faithful accounts of all moneys received by him as such treasurer, and of all expenditures and disbursements thereof. He shall pay out the moneys received by him as such treasurer, on the order of the board of trustees, certified by their secretary. He shall keep accurate accounts of all persons having dealings with the institution for which he is treasurer. He shall collect the tuition fees due the same, and shall submit a full and proper statement of the finances of such institution, of its receipts and disbursements, at each of the regular meetings of the said board, and at such other times as said board may direct.

[S. L. 1890-91, Ch. 92, Sec. 16.]

BOARD OF VISITORS—DUTY.

Sec. 519. A board of visitors for said agricultural college, to consist of three persons, shall be appointed biennially, at the commencement of the college year by the governor of the state. It shall be the duty of the board of visitors for said institution to make a personal examination into the state and condition thereof and all its affairs, twice at least in each year, and report the result to the governor, suggesting such improvements as they may deem proper, which report shall be submitted to the legislature at its next session. Such visitors shall receive no compensation for their services.

[S. L. 1890-91, Ch. 92, Sec. 17.]

FUNDS—HOW INVESTED.

Sec. 520. During such time as the University of Wyoming shall be and remain the recipient of the funds donated by the United States government to the state, under the act of congress of March 2, 1887, establishing agricultural experiment stations, and the act of congress of Augast 30, 1890, applying certain moneys in aid of agricultural colleges, and all acts of congress amendatory thereof or supplemental thereto, the treasurer of the state shall, upon the order of the board of trustees of said university, invest all moneys in his hands derived or arising from the sale, disposal or rental of the lands or any of them, donated to this state by congress for the use and support of an agricultural college, in such securities and loans as may be unanimously approved by all the trustees present at any regular meeting of said board of trustees of said university, provided, however, that no profit or interest from said loans or investments shall be so paid over for the support of said institution as hereinafter provided, until all loss or losses if any, out of the principal of said funds shall be made good and restored out of the said profits and interest; said loans or investments to be made in the name of the state of Wyoming, for the use of the Agricultural College Fund, the proceeds and payments upon or derived from said loans or investments, both principal and interest to be paid into the treasury of the state for the use of said fund, the principal for reinvestment and the profit and interest for the use of said college as herein provided.

[S. L. 1899, Ch. 13, Sec. 1.]

LIMITATION UPON INVESTMENT.

Sec. 521. Said fund shall be invested in bonds of the United States, of this state, or in bonds yielding not less than five per centum per annum upon the par value thereof issued by any county, municipal corporation or school district of this state.

[S. L. 1899, Ch. 13, Sec. 2.]

INTEREST—HOW USED.

Sec. 522. The net interest and profit received and derived from any loan or investment made in pursuance of the authority conferred by the last preceding section after all loss or losses have been made good as aforesaid shall, at all times, be available for use and may be used by the board of trustees of said university for any purpose connected with the supporting and maintenance of the Agricultural college at the University of Wyoming, not inconsistent or in conflict with any act of congress herein referred to, or any act amendatory thereof or supplemental thereto.

[S. L. 1899, Ch. 13, Sec. 3.]

CHAPTER 3.

PUBLIC SCHOOLS.

ARTICLE I.

SCHOOL DISTRICTS—ORGANIZATION AND POWERS.

NOTICE OF FORMATION OF NEW DISTRICT.

Sec. 523. Whenever a school district shall be formed in any county, the county superintendent of schools in such county shall, within fifteen days thereafter, prepare a notice of the formation of such district, describing its boundaries and stating the number thereof, and appointing a time and place for the district meeting. He shall cause the notice, thus prepared, to be posted in at least five public places in the district, at least ten days before the time appointed for such meeting; and when a joint district is derived from portions of two or more counties, the county superintendent of each county, from which any portion of the new district is taken, shall unite in giving the customary notices, and the new district shall be numbered by the superintendent of the county having the highest number of districts.

Baldwin vs. Wickman, 3 Wyo. 208.

[R. S. 1887, Sec. 3918.]

APPEAL FROM SUPERINTENDENT ON FORMATION OF DISTRICT.

Sec. 524. A majority of the voters in any school district, being dissatisfied with the formation of any school district, shall have the right to appeal from the superintendent to the board of county commissioners, and from the board of county commissioners to the superintendent of public instruction.

[R. S. 1887, Sec. 3919.]

FIRST ELECTION OF TRUSTEES—OFFICERS OF DISTRICT.

Sec. 525. The qualified electors of a school district when assembled in accordance with the notice required in section five hundred and twenty-three, shall organize by appointing a chairman and a secretary who shall act as judges of election.

—(2)

They shall then by ballot elect three trustees possessing the qualifications of electors of said district, and the name of each elector shall be recorded by the secretary and they shall hold their office until the next succeeding annual district election and until their successors are elected and qualified. The said trustees shall constitute a board of directors for the district and shall, as soon as they are qualified, choose from their number a director, treasurer and clerk of the district.

[S. L. 1890, Ch. 77, Sec. 1.]

ELECTION OF TRUSTEES WHERE NUMBER INCREASED TO SIX.

Sec. 526. In all school districts in this state containing a population of one thousand or more, the number of trustees may be increased to six at any annual school election held hereafter if the majority of the electors at such annual meeting, upon taking a vote by ballot so decide. The electors shall then proceed by ballot to elect one trustee for one year, one trustee for two years and two trustees for three years. At all annual elections held thereafter there shall be elected two trustees who shall hold their office for three years or until their successors are elected and qualified.

[S. L. 1897, Ch. 38.]

SCHOOL DISTRICT SEAL.

Sec. 527. It shall be the duty of every board of school directors so increased to six members, to provide at the expense of their district, and for said district, a seal, upon which shall be engraved the words "School District No. ...., ... County, Wyo.," stating the number of the district and the county in which it is situated. The seal shall be in possession of the clerk of the district. It shall be affixed to all communications or notices required by law to be sent or published by such school board, and to all warrants drawn upon the treasurer of the district.

[R. S. 1887, Sec. 3923.]

OATH OF DIRECTORS.

Sec. 528. All directors of the board shall, within ten days after their election, appear before some justice of the peace or other person qualified to administer oaths, and take an oath for the faithful performance of their duties and in accordance with law and shall, witout delay, transmit a copy of said oath in writing to the county superintendent of schools.

[S. L. 1890, Ch. 77, Sec. 2.]

SCHOOL DISTRICT TO BE BODY CORPORATE.

Sec. 529. Each school district formed under the provisions of this title, is hereby declared to be a body corporate by the name and style of "School District No. ...., in the County of ...., and State of Wyoming;" and in that name it may hold property, and be a party to suits and contracts.

[R. S. 1887, Sec. 3925.]

Powder River Cattle Co. vs. Board Commissioners, 3 Wyo. 597.

REGULAR MEETINGS OF DISTRICT.

Sec. 530. The regular meeting of each school district shall be held on the first Monday of May of each year. And, when present, the director and clerk shall preside as chairman and secretary of such meeting.

[R. S. 1887, Sec. 3926.]

POWERS OF DISTRICT MEETING.

Sec. 531. The qualified electors of the district, when assembled, shall have power:

1. To appoint a chairman and secretary, in the absence of the regular officers.

2. To adjourn from time to time, as occasion may require.

18

3. To determine the number of schools which shall be established in the district, and the length of time each shall be taught.

4. To fix the site of each school house, taking into consideration in doing so, the wants and necessities of the people of each portion of the district.

5. To vote such sum of money as the meeting shall deem sufficient for any of the following purposes: To supply any deficiency in the fund for the payment of teachers; to purchase or lease a suitable site for a school house, or school houses; to build, rent or purchase a school house or school houses, and keep in repair and furnish the same with the necessary fuel and appendages; for procuring libraries for the schools, books and stationery for the use of the board and district meetings; and for the payment of all other contingent expenses of the district; Provided, That the sum of money so voted shall not exceed ten mills on the dollar of all taxable property in each school district; Provided further, That the tax to be levied and collected, as authorized by this section, shall not exceed five mills on the dollar of the assessed valuation of the taxable property in any one year in all school districts having a total valuation of property exceeding three millions of dollars, or a valuation thereof of less than two hundred thousand dollars.

6. To direct the sale or other disposition to be made of any school house, or the site thereof, and of such other property, real or personal, as may belong to the district; and to direct the manner in which the proceeds arising therefrom shall be applied.

7. To vote a sum not exceeding one hundred dollars in any one year, to procure a district library, consisting of such books as they may direct any person to procure.

8. To delegate any and all powers specified in the foregoing subdivisions to the district board, provided that the district board shall not have power to vote or raise money as provided in sub-division five.

9. To transact generally such business as may tend to promote the cause of education in accordance with the provisions of this title.

[R. S. 1887, Sec. 3927.   S. L. 1888, Ch. 72, Sec. 12.   S. L. 1890, Ch. 77, Sec. 5.]
Miller vs. School District, 5 Wyo. 217.
School District vs. Western Tube Co., 5 Wyo. 185.

OBJECTS IN VOTING MONEY TO BE DESIGNATED.

Sec. 532. In voting money, the district meetings shall designate the respective objects for which the same is raised, and the amount to be raised for each object, and the aggregate amount shall be assessed and collected, as provided in this title.

[R. S. 1887, Sec. 3928.]
School District vs. Western Tube Co., 5 Wyo. 185.

MEETING MAY ADOPT RULES OF ORDER.

Sec. 533. They may adopt rules of order, not incompatible with the provisions of this chapter and the instructions of the superintendent of public instruction, for the government of district meetings, and may alter and change the some from time to time as occasion may require, and may prescribe the manner of taking the sense of the meeting upon any question; Provided, That the last specification shall not apply to the election of officers.

[R. S. 1887, Sec. 3929.]

TRANSFER OF SCHOOL FUNDS.

Sec. 534. In all cases where there are moneys belonging to the school house fund, remaining in the hands of the district treasurer of any school district, and the board of directors thereof are satisfied that such moneys are not required to build a school house or school houses, in said district, or repair or furnish the same, such moneys may be transferred and accredited to the teachers' fund, and applied to the payment of teachers. And the board may also in like manner transfer a surplus of the teachers' fund to the fund for building school houses when required.

[R. S. 1887, Sec. 3930.]

MANNER OF CONDUCTING ELECTION OF TRUSTEES.

Sec. 535. At the regular district meeting of school districts in each year, at the time now provided by law for the election of trustees, such district meeting shall be opened by proclamation of the trustees, at the hour named in the published or posted notice for the meeting. And the order of business at such meeting shall be:

1. Reading and consideration of the report of the clerk and treasurer.
2. Voting of money to be raised by special tax.
3. Election of trustee or trustees.
4. Miscellaneous business.

[S. L. 1888, Ch. 73, Sec. 1.]

Powder River Cattle Co. vs. Board Commissioners, 3 Wyo. 597.

QUALIFICATIONS OF ELECTORS.

Sec. 536. All school district elections shall be carried on as provided by law, and the qualifications of voters at such elections shall be the same as at any other election.

[S. L. 1890, Ch. 80, Sec. 179.]

ANNUAL ELECTION OF TRUSTEES—DISTRICT OFFICERS.

Sec. 537. Except as otherwise provided by law there shall be elected in each organized school district at the regular annual district meeting on the first Monday in May of each year, one trustee, who shall hold his office for three years and until his successor is duly elected and qualified. If, for any cause, the annual election should not be held at the regular annual meeting, a special meeting may be held for that purpose if so specified in the notice for said special meeting. The trustees together shall constitute a board of directors for the district, and shall, immediately after they are qualified, elect one of their number a director, treasurer and clerk of the district. At the first regular annual election after a school district is organized there shall be three trustees elected, one to hold his office for the term of three years, and one to hold his office for the term of two years, and one for the term of one year and until their successors are elected and qualified, and thereafter at each such annual meeting there shall be one trustee elected as aforesaid, for the term of three years as successor to the out-going member of the board, and all of said trustees herein mentioned shall possess the qualifications of any elector in said district, and shall be elected by ballot, and the name of each elector voting for trustee shall be recorded by the secretary of the meeting, and such record shall be filed with the district clerk..

[S. L. 1890, Ch. 77, Sec. 3.]

DIRECTORS SHALL QUALIFY.

Sec. 538. Said directors shall qualify in the manner prescribed for directors elected upon the formation of a new school district; and in case they neglect or refuse so to do, they shall be subject to the same penalty.

[R. S. 1887, Sec. 3934.]

MEETINGS OF BOARD.

Sec. 539. The board of directors may hold such regular, special or adjourned meetings as they may from time to time determine.

[R. S. 1887, Sec. 3935.]

POWERS AND DUTIES OF DISTRICT BOARD.

Sec. 540. The district board shall make all contracts, purchases, payments and sales, necessary to carry out every vote of the district, for procuring any site for a school house, renting, repairing or furnishing the same, and disposing thereof, or for keeping a school therein, and performing such other duties as may be delegated to them by the district meeting.

[R. S. 1887, Sec. 3936.]

School District vs. Western Tube Co., 5 Wyo. 185.

MEMBERS OF BOARD MAY ADMINISTER OATHS.

Sec. 541. The trustees of school districts are hereby severally authorized to administer oaths within their respective counties in any and all matters pertaining to their respective districts and the business thereof, where an oath is or shall be required by law.

[S. L. 1897, Ch. 4.]

AUTHORITY OF BOARD TO REMOVE SCHOLARS.

Sec. 542. The district board shall have power to admit scholars from adjoining districts, and remove scholars for disorderly conduct; and when scholars are admitted from other districts the district board may, in their discretion, require a tuition fee from such scholars.

[R. S. 1887, Sec. 3937.]

WHEN BOARD TO ADVERTISE FOR BIDS.

Sec. 543. Whenever any school house is to be built or any repairs, addition or improvement costing more than two hundred dollars made to any school house or district property, the board of directors of the district shall advertise for bids for such work, and in all cases contract the same to the lowest responsible bidder.

[R. S. 1887, Sec. 3938.]

SETTLEMENT WITH TREASURER—REPORT TO DISTRICT MEETING.

Sec. 544. They shall, from time to time examine the books and accounts of the treasurer, and make settlement with him, and shall, at each regular meeting of the district, present to the same a full statement of the receipts and expenditures of the district, and such other matters as may be deemed important.

[R. S. 1887, Sec. 3939.]

VISITING COMMITTEE.

Sec. 545. They shall appoint a committee from their own body to visit the respective schools of the district monthly, and to aid the teachers in establishing and enforcing rules for the government of schools, and see that the teachers keep a correct list of the pupils, the time which they attend school, the branches of learning which each is studying, and such other matters as may, in the opinion of the board, tend to promote the welfare of the school.

[R. S. 1887, Sec. 3940.]

AUDITING AND PAYMENT OF CLAIMS.

Sec. 546. They shall audit and allow all just claims against the district, and the directors shall draw an order for all demands thus audited, on the district treasurer.

[R. S. 1887, Sec. 3941.]

SPECIAL DISTRICT MEETINGS—REQUISITES OF NOTICE.

Sec. 547. They shall, upon the written request of five legal voters of the district, or whenever they deem it expedient, call special meetings thereof; but in all such cases, the notice of such meeting shall clearly state the precise object for which it is called, and time and place at which it is to be held.

[R. S. 1887, Sec. 3942.]

TERM OF EXISTING APPOINTEES TO FILL VACANCIES.

Sec. 548. In case a vacancy in any district school board, caused by the resignation, death or otherwise of any one of its members, is or has been filled by appointment, said appointee may legally hold such office until the next annual school election following said appointment, but no longer, and at the annual election said vacancy shall be filled in the same way and manner as authorized by law for the annual election of school trustees.

[R. S. 1887, Sec. 3943.]

VACANCY IN BOARD—HOW FILLED.

Sec. 549. When a vacancy occurs in any school board by the resignation, death or otherwise of any of its members, three months or more before the following annual school election, said vacancy cannot be filled by appointment, but a special election must be called in the way provided by law for the purpose of filling such vacancy; but if such vacancy occurs less than three months before the next annual school election, such vacancy shall be filled by appointment by the board.

[R. S. 1887, Sec. 3944.]

BOND OF DISTRICT TREASURER.

Sec. 550. The district treasurer shall give bonds to the district in such penalty and with such sureties as the board of the county commissioners shall direct and approve, conditioned for the faithful application of all money which may come into his hands by virtue of his office; Provided, Said bonds shall not exceed one and one-quarter times the amount of all the school moneys handled by such treasurer in any one year. Said penalty may be increased from time to time as the interests of the district may require. The said bond, after being approved by the board of county commissioners, shall be filed with the county treasurer, and it is hereby made unlawful for the county treasurer to pay over any sums of money out of the school fund to any district treasurer until such bond shall have been approved and filed as herein provided, and in case of a breach in the conditions of said bond, suit shall be brought thereon by the board of the county commissioners of the county in which the district is situated for the benefit of said district.

[R. S. 1887, Sec. 3945.]

ESTABLISHMENT OF HIGH SCHOOLS.

Sec. 551. The county superintendent and district board of directors may determine whether a school of a higher grade shall be established in the district, the number of teachers to be employed, and the course of instruction to be pursued therein, until the meeting of the teachers' institute, provided for by law, at which time the institute shall determine the studies to be pursued in all schools of like grade in the state; and the superintendent of public instruction shall have the same power to carry into effect the determination of the institute, as is provided in other cases; and the board may erect, for the purpose, one or more permanent school houses, and shall cause such classification of the pupils as they may deem necessary; but in selecting the site for such school house or school houses the permanent interest and future welfare of the people of the entire district shall be consulted.

[R. S. 1887, Sec. 3946.]

SEPARATE SCHOOL FOR COLORED CHILDREN.

Sec. 552. When there are fifteen or more colored children within any school district, the board of directors thereof, with the approval of the county superintendent of schools, may provide a separate school for the instruction of such colored children.

[R. S. 1887, Sec. 3947.]

EMPLOYMENT AND PAYMENT OF TEACHERS.

Sec. 553.   The district board shall employ all teachers necessary for the schools of the district, and pay them by draft on the treasurer.

[R. S. 1887, Sec. 3948.]

SCHOOL AGE—COMPULSORY EDUCATION.

Sec. 554. The district schools established under the provisions of this title shall at all times be equally free and accessible to all children resident therein, over six and under the age of twenty-one years, subject to such regulations as the district board in each district may prescribe. And it shall be the duty of all parents and guardians or other persons having the control of children between the ages above mentioned, to send such children to some school, at least three months in each and every year, except in case of invalids, and others to whom the school room would be injurious. In such cases, the district board shall, upon receipt of a physician's certificate, excuse such children; and the district board may, in its discretion, excuse children from attendance when a compliance with this title would work great hardship. In all such cases the clerk of the board shall state the reason for excuse, and the name of the child or person excused, and the length of time for which excused, at large in the minutes of the proceedings of the board. Provided, That in all cases the applicant may appeal from the decision of the board to the county superintendent, whose decision shall be final.

[R. S. 1887, Sec. 3949.]

LIABILITY OF PARENTS AND GUARDIANS—AUTHORITY OF POLICE OFFICERS.

Sec. 555. Any parent or guardian, or other person, having children in their charge between the ages of seven and sixteen years, who shall neglect or refuse to comply with the provisions of this chapter, shall, on conviction, be punished by a fine not exceeding twenty-five dollars, for each and every offense, and it shall be the duty of all sheriffs, constables or police officers, at all times, whenever it comes to their knowledge that any child is living idly and loitering about the streets or thoroughfares and spending its time in an idle and dissolute manner, to notify some member of the school board of the district in which such child is living, whose duty it shall be to immediately make all the proper inquiries to ascertain the reasons for the non-attendance of said child in some school of the county in which such child may be found by said board. If any such child or ward is wilfully violating the conditions of this law, it shall become the duty of the county superintendent of schools, on written notice from the board, to make a complaint before some justice of the peace against the parent or guardian of said child or ward, or to make complaint against such child or ward, as provided in cases of vagrancy, under the laws of this state.

[R. S. 1887, Sec. 3950.]

ARTICLE II.

DISTRICT OFFICERS AND THEIR DUTIES.

DIRECTOR TO PRESIDE AT MEETINGS AND COUNTERSIGN ORDERS.

Sec. 556. The director, when present, shall preside at all meetings of the board of the district, and countersign all orders on the treasury for the payment of money.

[R. S. 1887, Sec. 3951.]

HOW DRAFTS AND ORDERS DRAWN.

Sec. 557. All drafts and orders drawn on the district treasurer, as required in the foregoing section, shall specify the fund on which they are drawn, and the use for which the money is designed, and shall be signed by the district clerk.

[R. S. 1887, Sec. 3952.]

BY WHOM DISTRICT TO APPEAR IN ACTIONS.

Sec. 558. The director shall appear in behalf of his district in all suits brought by or against the same; but when he is individually a party, this duty shall be performed by the clerk.

[R. S. 1887, Sec. 3953.]

DUTIES OF CLERK.

Sec. 559. The clerk shall record all the proceedings of the board and of the district meetings in books to be kept for that purpose, and report in writing to the county superintendent of schools the name of the director and treasurer immediately after they are chosen or elected, and he shall preserve copies of all reports made to the county superintendent, and shall file all papers transmitted to him, by school officers or other persons, pertaining to the business of the district, and shall sign all drafts, warrants and orders drawn by him.

[S. L. 1890, Ch. 77, Sec. 4.]

CLERK TO CERTIFY DEBT LIMIT.

Sec. 560. The clerk of each school district of each county shall endorse a certificate upon every bond or evidence of debt issued pursuant to law, that the same is within the lawful debt limit of such school district, and is issued according to law. He shall sign such certificate in his official character.

[S. L. 1890-91, Ch. 43, Sec. 2.]

CLERKS SHALL KEEP ACCOUNTS.

Sec. 561. The district clerk shall keep an accurate account of all the expenses incurred by the district, and shall present the same to the district board, to be audited and paid as herein provided, out of the school fund.

[R. S. 1887, Sec. 3955.]

NOTICE OF DISTRICT MEETINGS.

Sec. 562. The district clerk shall give ten days previous notice of all regular and special meetings of the district, herein authorized, by posting up a written notice in three different places therein; and shall furnish a copy of the same to the teachers of each school in the district, to be read once in the presence of the pupils thereof.

[R. S. 1887, Sec. 3956.]

24

ANNUAL REPORT OF CLERK TO COUNTY SUPERINTENDENT.

Sec. 563. The district clerk shall, on the first Monday of September in each year, submit a report to the county superintendent, for the year past, then ending:

1. Of the number of schools taught in such district, the number of days each scholar attended the same, and the aggregate number of days of attendance of said school respectively, as certified by the teachers of the several schools of such district.

2. The number of schools and the branches taught in each.

3. The number of pupils in each school, and of each sex.

4. The number of teachers employed in each school, and the average compensation of each per month.

5. The number of days the school has been taught, and by whom.

6. The average cost of tuition for a pupil, per month, in each school.

7. Books used in each school.

8. The number of volumes in the library of each school.

9. The aggregate amount paid teachers during the year, the source from which the same was received, and the amount of the teachers' fund in the hands of the treasurer.

10. The number of district school houses, and the cost of each.

11. The amount raised in the district by tax, for the erection of school houses, and for other purposes authorized in this title, and such other information as he may deem useful.

[R. S. 1887, Sec. 3957.]

FAILURE TO MAKE REPORT—PENALTY.

Sec. 564. Should the clerk fail to file his report, as above directed, he shall forfeit the sum of twenty-five dollars, and shall be liable to make good all loss resulting to the district from such failure, suit to be brought in both cases by the director, in the name of the district, on his official bond.

[R. S. 1887, Sec. 3958.]

DUTIES OF TREASURER—PUBLICATION OF REPORT.

Sec. 565. The treasurer shall have the custody of all moneys belonging to the district, and shall pay out the same upon the order of the clerk, countersigned by the director; and shall keep an account of the receipts and expenditures thereof, in a book provided for that purpose. He shall cause to be published in some newspaper of general circulation in the county wherein such school district is situate, on the first week of July in each year, a full and true report of the receipts and disbursements of said district for the year next preceding such report.

[R. S. 1887, Sec. 3959.]

TEACHERS' FUND.

Sec. 566. The moneys for the payment of teachers shall be called the "teachers' fund," and the treasurer shall keep distinct and separate accounts with them; and no warrant for money shall be paid by the treasurer which does not specify the fund on which it is drawn, and the specific use to which it is to be applied.

[R. S. 1887, Sec. 3960.]

School District vs. Western Tube Co., 5 Wyo. 185.

SCHOOL HOUSE FUND.

Sec. 567. The school house fund shall consist only of taxes collected in the district; and all other school moneys belonging to the district shall go to the teachers' fund, and shall be applied to no other use except to pay the wages of school teachers in the district.

[R. S. 1887, Sec. 3961.]

25

TREASURER TO RECEIVE DISTRICT MONEY.

Sec. 568. The district treasurer shall apply for, and receive all money apportioned to the district, by the county superintendent, when notified of said apportionment.

[R. S. 1887, Sec. 3962.]

TREASURER TO RENDER STATEMENT ON REQUEST.

Sec. 569. The district treasurer shall render a statement of the finances of the district as shown by the records of his office, at any time when required by the district board.

[R. S. 1887, Sec. 3963.]

ARTICLE III.

SCHOOL DISTRICT BONDS.

AUTHORITY TO CALL ELECTION TO DETERMINE ISSUE.

Sec. 570. The board of school trustees of any school district may, whenever a majority thereof so decide, submit to the electors of the district the question whether the board shall be authorized to issue the coupon bonds of the district to a certain amount, not to exceed two per cent. of the taxable property in said district, and bearing a certain rate of interest, not exceeding six per cent. per annum, and payable and redeemable at a certain time, not exceeding twenty-five years, for the purpose of building one or more school houses in said district, and providing the same with necessary furniture, and funding outstanding indebtedness evidenced by warrant or otherwise, against said district.

[S. L. 1897, Ch. 41.]

BOND ELECTION—ISSUE OF BONDS.

Sec. 571. Such elections must be held in the manner prescribed for general or special elections in school districts, and the ballots must contain the words "Bonds, yes;" or "bonds, no." If the majority of the votes at such election are, "bonds, yes," the board of trustees must issue such bonds in such form as the board may direct; they must bear the signatures of the president of the board of trustees and be countersigned by the clerk of the school district, and bear the district seal and be countersigned by the county treasurer, and the coupon attached to the bonds must be signed by the president and clerk and the county treasurer. And each bond so issued must be registered by the county treasurer in a book provided for that purpose, which must show the number and amount of each bond, and the person to whom the same is issued, and the said bonds must be sold by the said school trustees, as provided in section five hundred and seventy-two.

[S. L. 1888, Ch. 72, Sec. 2.]

SALE OF BONDS—APPLICATION OF PROCEEDS.

Sec. 572. The school trustees must give notice in some newspaper of general circulation, published in the capital of this state, and also in some newspaper published in the county in which said school district is located, for a period of not less than four weeks, to the effect that the said school trustees will sell said bonds, briefly describing the same, and the time and place where such sale will take place; Provided, That the said bonds must not be sold for less than their par value, and the said trustees are authorized to reject any bids, and to sell said bonds at private sale, if they deem it for the best interests of the district; and all money arising from the sale of said bonds must be paid forthwith into the treasury of the county in which said district may be located, to the credit of said district, and the same shall be immediately available for the purpose of building or providing the school house, or school houses authorized by this chapter.

PLEDGE FOR PAYMENT.
[S. L. 1888, Ch. 72, Sec. 3.]

Sec. 573. The faith of each school district is solemnly pledged for the payment of the interest, and the redemption of the principal of all bonds which are issued under this chapter.

TAX LEVY TO REDEEM AND PAY INTEREST.
[S. L. 1888, Ch. 72, Sec. 4.]

Sec. 574. The board of county commissioners of the proper county of each district must ascertain and levy annually, the tax necessary to pay the interest as it becomes due, and a sinking fund to redeem the said bonds at their maturity; and said tax is a lien upon the property in said school district, and must be collected in the same manner as other taxes for school purposes. Said tax shall be known as "district bond tax of school district No. . . . ."

REDEMPTION.
[S. L. 1888, Ch. 72, Sec. 5.]

Sec. 575. When the sum in the sinking fund equals or exceeds the amount of any bond then due, the county treasurer shall post in his office, a notice that he will, within thirty days from the date of such notice, redeem the bonds then payable, giving the number thereof, and the preference must be given to the oldest issue; and if, at the expiration of the said thirty days, the holder or holders of said bonds, shall fail or neglect to present the same for payment, interest thereon must cease; but the treasurer shall, at all times thereafter, be ready to redeem the same on presentation, and when any bonds are so purchased or redeemed, the county treasurer must cancel the same by writing across the face of each bond in red ink, the word, "cancelled," and the date of such cancellation. The annual interest on all of said bonds shall be payable at the office of the treasurer of the proper county on the first and ten succeeding days of January in each year.

PAYMENT OF INTEREST.
[S. L. 1888, Ch. 72, Sec. 6.]

Sec. 576. The county treasurer may pay out of any moneys belonging to a school district tax fund, the interest upon any bonds issued under this chapter by such school district, when the same becomes due, upon the presentation at his office of the proper coupon, which must show the amount due, and the number of the bond to which it belonged, and all coupons so paid, must be reported to the school trustees at their first regular meeting thereafter.

PREPARATION OF BONDS.
[S. L. 1888, Ch. 72, Sec. 7.]

Sec. 577. The school trustees of any district, shall cause to be printed or lithographed at the lowest rates, suitable bonds, with the coupons attached, when the same become necessary, and pay therefor out of any moneys in their treasury.

[S. L. 1888, Ch. 72, Sec. 8.]
PENALTY FOR MISAPPLICATION OF FUNDS BY TRUSTEES.

Sec. 578. If any of the school trustees fraudulently fail or refuse

27

to pay into the proper county treasury the money arising from the sale of any bonds provided for by this chapter, they shall be deemed guilty of felony, and upon conviction thereof, be punished by imprisonment in the state penitentiary for a term of not less than one year, nor more than ten years.

[S. L. 1888, Ch. 72, Sec. 9.]

COUNTY TREASURER SHALL HAVE CUSTODY OF FUNDS.

Sec. 579. The county treasurer of such county shall have the custody of all funds realized from the sale of said bonds, until the same are drawn out by the order of the board of directors of said district.

[S. L. 1888, Ch. 72, Sec. 10.]

ADDITIONAL BOND OF COUNTY TREASURER.

Sec. 580. The board of trustees of said district shall require the said county treasurer to give said district a separate bond in such sum as said board may deem proper, with two or more sufficient sureties, conditioned for the faithful performance of the duties required of him by this act, and the faithful accounting for the moneys deposited with him and realized from the sale of said bonds, as herein provided for, and such bonds shall be approved by said board and shall be and remain in the custody of said board of trustees.

[S. L. 1888, Ch. 72, Sec. 11.]

ARTICLE IV.

REFUNDING SCHOOL DISTRICT BONDS.

POWER OF BOARD TO ISSUE REFUNDING BONDS.

Sec. 581. The board of directors of each and every school district in the state of Wyoming are hereby authorized to issue refunding bonds of such school district, for the purpose of taking up outstanding bonds of such school district, for any sum not exceeding the amount of outstanding bonds; Provided, That the qualified electors of any school district shall so elect and determine at any regular meeting, or at any special meeting, held for such purpose.

[S. L. 1893, Ch. 10, Sec. 1.]

Miller vs. School District, 5 Wyo. 217.

FORM OF BOND, TIME AND INTEREST.

Sec. 582. Said bonds shall be issued in sums of not less than one hundred dollars, and shall be redeemed by the school district issuing the same within a period not exceeding thirty years, and not less than five years from the date of issue, and shall bear interest at a rate not exceeding six per centum per annum, on each dollar of their face, which interest shall be payable annually or semi-annually, the rate of interest to be determined by the board of school directors. Such bonds shall be numbered from one upwards, and be headed "Refunding bonds of school district number ...., in the county of ...., state of Wyoming;" and before being issued shall be registered by the treasurer of the county, within which such school district is situated.

[S. L. 1893, Ch. 10, Sec. 2.]

REGISTRATION OF BOND.

Sec. 583. The county treasurer of each county shall keep a book in which shall be registered all such bonds, showing the number of the bond, the date of issue, amount, number of coupons, date of redemption, date of registry and payment of interest on such bonds, which book shall, during business hours, be open for inspection.

[S. L. 1893, Ch. 10, Sec. 3.]

BY WHOM SIGNED AND SALE THEREOF.

Sec. 584. All bonds so issued shall be signed by the presiding officer of the board of directors of such school district, countersigned by the county treasurer of the county in which such school district is situated, and attested by the clerk of such school district, with the seal of such school district attached; and none of such bonds shall be sold for less than their face value, and shall not be sold until thirty days notice shall have been given in some newspaper of general circulation in the state of Wyoming.

[S. L. 1893, Ch. 10, Sec. 4.]

COUPONS—WHERE PAID.

Sec. 585. Said bonds shall have coupons attached, representing the interest to be paid each year, and the coupons representing said interest shall be detached from the bonds before presentation for payment of the interest for the year corresponding, and upon payment shall be forthwith cancelled by the county treasurer, by writing the word "cancelled" across the face thereof. The interest on all such bonds shall be payable at the office of the county treasurer of the county in which such school district issuing such bonds is situated, or in any place designated by the board of school directors of such school district.

[S. L. 1893, Ch. 10, Sec. 5.]

TAX TO PAY INTEREST AND PRINCIPAL.

Sec. 586. There shall be annually levied by the board of county commissioners of the county, within which is situate any school district issuing any such bonds, as are herein provided for, on all taxable property within the limits of said school district, a tax not to exceed seven mills on the dollar of valuation, which shall be know as the "Refunding Bond Fund of school district No.........." Said tax shall be payable only in the lawful money of the United States, and shall be used to pay the interest and principal of said bonds, and for no other purpose; and said tax shall be collected in the same manner. and at the same time as the county taxes, and paid into the county treasury by the collector of taxes.

[S. L. 1893, Ch. 10, Sec. 6.]

DUTY OF SCHOOL DIRECTORS AS TO REDEMPTION.

Sec. 587. The board of school directors of any school district, which may issue bonds, as provided in this article, shall each year, after the tenth year, retire as many of such bonds as can be redeemed, with the amount of said bond fund, at the time in the hands of the county treasurer, and in all such cases, such bonds shall be redeemed by the payment of number one first, and proceeding continuously upwards with those outstanding. All cancelled bonds shall be turned over to the board of directors at such times as they may direct.

[S. L. 1893, Ch. 10, Sec. 7.]

PROPERTY IN DISTRICT PLEDGED FOR PAYMENT.

Sec. 588. All taxable property of any school.district issuing bonds, as herein provided for, at the time of issuing such bonds, shall be pledged for the payment of the principal and interest of such bonds in the

29

manner herein provided, and it shall not be lawful to use or divert any portion of such bond fund for any purpose whatever, except for the payment of such principal and interest.

[S. L. 1893, Ch. 10, Sec. 8.]

DUTY OF COUNTY TREASURER.

Sec. 589. The county treasurer of each county in which any school district, issuing bonds as herein provided for, is situated, shall have custody of all funds realized from the sale of such bonds, and shall pay the same out only upon the return of such bonds, for the redemption of which the refunding bonds, for the issue of which this article provides, may have been issued. Such bonds so redeemed shall be cancelled by the county treasurer and turned over to the board of school directors of the school district which issued said redeemed bonds at such time as they may direct. It shall be the duty of the county treasurer to give a separate bond to be made to such school district, in such sum and with such sureties as the board of county commissioners of the county may deem proper and sufficient, conditioned for the faithful accounting of the moneys deposited with him and realized from the sale of such bonds as are herein provided for, and such treasurer's separate bond shall be and remain in the custody of the county clerk of the county in which such school district is situated.

[S. L. 1893, Ch. 10, Sec. 9.]

FUNDS REALIZED FROM SALE OF REFUNDING BONDS.

Sec. 590. Whenever any school district shall have issued its refunding bonds, and the funds realized from the sale of such refunding bonds, by reason of such bonds selling for more than their par value, are more than sufficient to redeem all the bonds, to redeem which said refunding bonds were issued, such surplus may be used, First. To pay all the expense of issuing and disposing of said refunding bonds. Second. Any surplus still remaining shall be turned by the county treasurer into the "Refunding Bond Fund" of such school district, and used for the purposes for which such fund is used as provided in section five hundred and eighty-six.

[S. L. 1895, Ch. 10, Sec. 1.]

BALANCE IN THE HANDS OF COUNTY TREASURER—HOW USED.

Sec. 591. Whenever any school district shall have issued its refunding bonds and there remains in the hands of the county treasurer of the county in which said school district is situated, any moneys belonging to the funds provided by law for the payment of the principal or interest, or both, of the bonds to redeem which said refunding bonds were issued, said money may be used, First. To pay any deficiency in the expenses of issuing and disposing of said refunding bonds that cannot be paid by the surplus realized from the sale of said refunding bonds. Second. Any moneys still remaining in said fund shall be turned by said county treasurer into the "Refunding Bond Fund" of such school district and used for the purposes for which such fund is used as provided in section five hundred and eighty-six.

[S. L. 1895, Ch. 10, Sec. 2.]

SURPLUS—HOW USED.

Sec. 592. The county treasurer of any county in which is situated a school district that may issue refunding bonds, is hereby authorized and required to pay out the surplus moneys derived from the sale of any such refunding bonds, or the surplus moneys remaining in the old fund for the expenses incurred by such school district in issuing and disposing of such refunding bonds on orders of the school board of such school district, which orders shall state on their face that the money to be so paid was a legitimate expense incurred in the issue and sale of such refunding bonds. When all of such expense has been paid by the issue of such orders or otherwise, the board of directors shall, over the seal of said district, notify said county treasurer of the fact that all the expense incurred in the issue and sale of such refunding bonds has been paid, whereupon said treasurer shall immediately transfer all moneys remaining in his hands applicable to the payment of interest or principal of the old bonds to the "Refunding Bond Fund" of such school district; Provided, however, That all the bonds to redeem which said refunding bonds were issued have already been paid.

[S. L. 1895, Ch. 10, Sec. 3.]

ARTICLE V.

PUBLIC KINDERGARTEN.

POWER OF TRUSTEES TO ESTABLISH KINDERGARTEN.

Sec. 593. The board of trustees of any school district in this state shall have power to establish and maintain free kindergarten schools in connection with the public schools of their district, for the instruction of children residing in such district and between the ages of four and six years, and shall establish such courses of training, study and discipline and such rules and regulations for the government of such kindergarten schools as said board may deem advisable; Provided, That the cost of establishing and maintaining such kindergarten schools shall be paid from the special school fund of said school district, and the gross sum to be so expended by the said board for such kindergarten schools shall be annually fixed and determined by the qualified electors of such district at the annual meeting of such electors.

[S. L. 1895, Ch. 50, Sec. 1.]

SHALL BE PART OF SCHOOL SYSTEM—TEACHERS.

Sec. 594. The said kindergarten schools shall be a part of the public school system and governed as far as practicable in the same manner and by the same officers as is now, or hereafter may be provided by law, for the government of the other public schools of this state; Provided, however, that teachers of the kindergarten schools shall be the holders of certificates or diplomas from some reputable institution for the training of kindergarten teachers, and shall pass such other examination and possess such other qualifications as may be required by the board of trustees of the district employing them.

[S. L. 1895, Ch. 50, Sec. 1.]

LAW NOT CHANGED IN REFERENCE TO APPORTIONMENT.

Sec. 595. Nothing in this article shall be so construed as to, in any manner, change the law, as it now exists, with reference to the taking of the census of the school population, or the apportionment of the state and county school funds among the several counties and districts in this state.

[S. L. 1895, Ch. 50, Sec. 1.]

HOW CARRIED INTO EFFECT.

Sec. 596. That for the purpose of carrying into effect the provisions of this article, it shall be lawful for the qualified electors of any school district in the state at the annual meeting held under the provisions of existing law, to vote such sum of money as may be necessary to establish and maintain such kindergarten schools, during the school year next following such meeting, such sum in the aggregate not to exceed one mill upon the dollar of the valuation of the property in the district, as determined by the next preceding annual assessment thereof for the purposes of taxation, the same to be certified, levied, collected and disbursed in the same manner as is now provided by law with respect to the special school funds of the several school districts in this state.

[S. L. 1895, Ch. 50, Sec. 2.]

ARTICLE VI.

FREE TEXT BOOKS.

DUTY OF SCHOOL DIRECTORS.

Sec. 597. Boards of school directors in city or county are hereby empowered, and it is made their duty, to purchase all text books necessary for the schools of such city, town or district; and they are further authorized to enter into contract, as hereinafter provided, with the publishers of such books for a term of years, not to exceed five; provided, that the contract prices of such books shall not exceed the lowest price then granted to any dealer, state, county, township, school district, or other individual or corporation in the United States, to be determined as hereinafter provided; and, provided further, that such contract shall guarantee to such districts any further reduction that may be granted elsewhere during the life of such contract.

[S. L. 1899, Ch. 29, Sec. 1.]

PUBLISHERS MUST FILE BOND.

Sec. 598. Before any publisher of school books shall be permitted to enter into contract with any school district under the provisions of this article, he shall file with the state superintendent of public instruction, to be approved by him, a good and sufficient bond in the sum of two thousand to twenty thousand dollars, which amount shall be fixed by the state superintendent of public instruction, for the faithful performance of the conditions of such contracts, and the observance of the requirements of this article; and such publisher shall also file with the state superintendent of public instruction, a sworn statement of the lowest prices for which his series of text books are sold anywhere in the United States; and a failure to file such bond and sworn statement of prices shall be a good and valid defense on the part of the district against payment for any books that may be sold by such publisher prior to the date of filing such bond and sworn statement of prices; and all such contracts to which such publisher is a party made prior to filing such bond and sworn statement of prices, shall be null and void.

[S. L. 1899, Ch. 29, Sec. 2.]

BOOKS—PAID FOR FROM PUBLIC SCHOOL LAND INCOME FUND.

Sec. 599. The books to be purchased under the provisions of this article shall be paid for by the directors of the different school districts of the state, out of the public school land income fund, when the same shall be distributed to such districts annually.

[S. L. 1899, Ch. 29, Sec. 11.]

BOOKS PAID FOR BY ORDER ON DISTRICT TREASURER. .

Sec. 600. For the purpose of paying for school books, the school district officers may draw an order on the district treasurer for the amount of school books ordered.

[S. L. 1899, Ch. 29, Sec. 3.]
ORDERS—FROM WHAT FUNDS PAID.

Sec. 601. The district treasurer shall pay orders drawn by school district officers for the purpose of school books out of any funds in his hands belonging to the district, except the money belonging to the teachers' fund.

[S. L. 1899, Ch. 29, Sec. 4.]
PUBLISHER BECOMING MEMBER OF TRUST NULLIFIES CONTRACT.

Sec. 602. Any contract entered into under the provisions of this article with any publisher who shall hereafter become a party to any combination or trust for the purpose of raising the price of school text books shall, at the wish of the school board of the district using such books, become null and void.

[S. L. 1899, Ch. 29, Sec. 5.]
DUTY SUPERINTENDENT OF PUBLIC INSTRUCTION.

Sec. 603. The state superintendent of public instruction shall, within thirty days after the filing of the hereinbefore mentioned sworn statement of prices of text books, have the same printed and forward a sufficient number of certified copies of the same to each of the county superintendents of the state to furnish all the school districts of such county with one copy each; and the county superintendent shall immediately after receiving said certified copies of prices of books send or deliver one of such certified copies to the directors or secretary of each school district or board of education in such county, to be filed as a part of the records of such district; and he shall also file one of said certified copies of prices in his office as a part of the records of said office.

[S. L. 1899, Ch. 29, Sec. 6.]
SUPERINTENDENT MUST FURNISH FORM OF CONTRACT.

Sec. 604. It shall be the duty of the state superintendent of public instruction to prepare and have printed a form of contract between district boards and publishers of school books and to furnish the same through the county superintendent to the several district boards of the state; and no other form of contract shall be used by such district boards and publishers.

[S. L. 1899, Ch. 29, Sec. 7.]
ATTORNEY GENERAL MUST INVESTIGATE VIOLATION OF CONTRACTS.

Sec. 605. Upon the filing of a written complaint with the state superintendent of public instruction by the officers of any district board, charging any publisher with violating the conditions of such contract as hereinbefore mentioned, the attorney general is hereby instructed, and it shall be his duty, to investigate the same, and if he finds probable cause for action, he shall immediately begin proceedings in the name of the state to enforce the liability on the bond hereinbefore mentioned.

[S. L. 1899, Ch. 29, Sec. 8.]
BOOKS PROPERTY OF DISTRICT.

Sec. 606. All books purchased by district boards, as hereinbefore mentioned, shall be held as the property of the district, and loaned to pupils of the school while pursuing a course of study therein, free of charge; but the district boards shall hold such pupils responsible for any damage to, loss of, or failure to return such books at the time and to the person that may be designated by the board of such district.

[S. L. 1899, Ch. 29, Sec. 9.]

PUPILS MAY PURCHASE BOOKS.

Sec. 607. The provisions of this article shall include all school supplies; provided, that nothing in this article shall be construed to prohibit any pupil or parent from purchasing from the board such books as may be necessary, at cost to the district; provided further, that the board may designate some local dealer to handle books for the district with such an increase above contract price to pay cost of transportation and handling, as may be agreed upon between said board and said dealer.

[S. L. 1899, Ch. 29, Sec. 10.]

ARTICLE VII.

MISCELLANEOUS PROVISIONS.

OFFENSES DEFINED—PENALTY.

Sec. 608. Any person who shall use insulting and abusive language to and toward any teacher in or about any public school house, or who shall wilfully disturb any public school or district meeting, shall be deemed guilty of a misdemeanor, and, upon conviction, shall be fined in any sum not less than five dollars, and not exceeding one hundred dollars.

Any person who shall wilfully break, cut, deface, despoil, injure, damage or destroy any school property, or who shall cut, mark, write or otherwise place or put on, or cause to be placed or put upon, any school property, any language or pictures or figures or signs of an obscene character, shall be deemed guilty of a misdemeanor, and, upon conviction thereof, shall pay a fine of not less than five dollars, nor more than one hundred dollars. The said fines shall be paid into the treasury of the school district in which the offense was committed.

[S. L. 1888, Ch. 72, Sub. Div. 2, Secs. 1-2.]

SCHOOL WEEK AND MONTH DEFINED.

Sec. 609. For the purposes of this chapter, a school week shall consist of five days; and a school month shall consist of all the days of a calendar month except Saturdays and Sundays, and legal holidays.

[S. L. 1888, Ch. 72, Sub. Div. 3, Sec. 1.]

SCHOOL OFFICERS SHALL NOT BE AGENTS FOR SCHOOL SUPPLIES—PENALTY.

Sec. 610. Neither the state superintendent, or any person in his office, nor any county superintendent, nor school district officer, nor any officer or teacher connected with any public school, shall act as agent or solicitor for the sale of any school books, maps, charts, school library books, school furniture, apparatus or stationery, or furnish any assistance to, or receive any reward therefor, from any author, publisher, bookseller or dealer, doing the same. Every person violating this section shall forfeit not less than fifty nor more than two hundred dollars for each offense, and be liable to removal from office therefor.

[S. L. 1888, Ch. 72, Sub. Div. 3, Sec. 2.]

STATE TREASURER SHALL KEEP SCHOOL FUND.

Sec. 611. The state treasurer shall keep a separate fund to be known as the "school fund," and all moneys appropriated for school purposes shall be kept in such fund.

[S. L. 1888, Ch. 72, Sub. Div. 3, Sec. 3.]

PHYSIOLOGY AND HYGIENE SHALL BE TAUGHT.

Sec. 612. Physiology and hygiene, which shall include in each division of the subject special reference to the effects of alcohol and narcotics upon the human system, shall be included in the branches taught in the common schools of the state, and shall be introduced and taught, either orally or by text book, in all departments of the public schools above the second primary grade, and in all educational institutions supported wholly or in part by the state.

[R. S. 1887, Sec. 3939.]

FAILURE TO COMPLY WITH LAST SECTION—PENALTY.

Sec. 613. It shall be the duty of the several county and city superintendents of schools in the state, and of the secretary of the board of directors of all other educational institutions receiving aid from the state, to report to the state superintendent of public instruction any failure or neglect on the part of the board of trustees of any school district, or the board of directors of any educational institution receiving aid from the state, to make proper provision for the teaching of the branches mentioned in the last preceding section in any or all of the schools or other educational institutions under their charge, or over which they have jurisdiction, and such failure on the part of the above mentioned officers, so reported and satisfactorily proved, shall be deemed sufficient cause for withholding the warrant for the district appropriation of school money to which such school district or educational institution would otherwise be entitled.

[R. S. 1887, Sec. 3970.]

DISCRIMINATION ON ACCOUNT OF SEX OR RELIGIOUS BELIEF PROHIBITED.

Sec. 614. In the employment of teachers in the public schools in this state, no discrimination shall be made in the question of pay on account of sex, nor on account of the religious belief of the applicant for the position of teacher, when the persons are equally qualified, and the labor is the same.

[S. L. 1890-91, Ch. 21.]

EXAMINATIONS REQUIRED.

Sec. 615. No certificate shall be granted hereafter to any person to teach in the schools of Wyoming, who shall not pass a satisfactory examination in physiology and hygiene, with special reference to the effects of alcoholic drinks, stimulants and narcotics upon the human system.

[R. S. 1887, Sec. 3972.]

35

TEACHER'S REPORT.

Sec. 616. It shall be the duty of the teacher of every district school, or graded school, to make out and file with the district clerk, at the expiration of each term of the school, a full report of the whole number of scholars admitted to the school during such term, distinguishing between male and female, the names of such scholars, the number of days each scholar attended the same, the aggregate number of days attendance of said schools, the text books used, the branches taught and the number of pupils engaged in the study of each of said branches. Any teacher who shall neglect or refuse to comply with the requirements of this section, shall forfeit his or her wages for teaching such school, at the discretion of the district board.

[R. S. 1887, Sec. 3973.]

People ex rel vs. Dolan, 5 Wyo. 245.

REFUSAL TO DELIVER RECORDS TO SUCCESSOR—PENALTY.

Sec. 617. Every school district clerk, or treasurer, who shall neglect or refuse to deliver to their successors in office, all records and books, belonging severally to their offices, shall be subject to a fine not exceeding five hundred dollars.

[R. S. 1887, Sec. 3974.]

EMPLOYMENT OF COUNSEL.

Sec. 618. In all cases where suits may be instituted, by, or against, any of the school officers contemplated or created by this title, to enforce any of the provisions herein contained, counsel may be employed, if necessary, by the officer instituting the suit, and the expense of the suit shall be borne by the district. county or state in whose name, or against whom, the same may be instituted.

[R. S. 1887, Sec. 3975.]

COLLECTION AND DISPOSITION OF FINES.

Sec. 619. All fines, penalties and forfeitures provided by this title may be recovered by action in the name of the people of the state of Wyoming for the use of the proper school district or county, and when they accrue, belong to the respective districts or counties in which the same may have accrued; and the treasurer of such districts, and the county commissioners of such counties are hereby authorized to receive and apply the proceeds of such forfeitures as the interest of the permanent fund is now, or may hereafter be, applied.

[R. S. 1887, Sec. 3976.]

People ex rel vs. Dolan, 5 Wyo. 245.

OFFICER FAILING TO PAY OVER MONEY—PENALTY.

Sec. 620. Any officer or person collecting or receiving any fines, forfeitures or other moneys and refusing and failing to pay over the same as required by law, shall forfeit double the amount so withheld, and interest thereon at the rate of five per cent. per month during the time of so withholding the same.

[R. S. 1887, Sec. 3977.]

People ex rel vs. Dolan, 5 Wyo. 245.

EFFECT OF CHANGE IN COUNTY BOUNDARIES ON SCHOOL DISTRICTS.

Sec. 621. If by any act of the state legislature changing the boundary line or lines of any county or counties, or forming new counties from counties already formed, any legally organized school district is or has been separated from the county to which it then belonged, and is or has been joined to another county, the members of the school board of such school district so separated from one county and joined to another county, shall hold their respective offices until the next annual school election following said change in county

boundaries; and until such annual school election said school board
may draw the public school funds for paying teachers, or other
necessary legal school expenses from the school treasury of the county
to which said school district formerly belonged, and in the same way and
manner as said board would have drawn and expended said public moneys
had no change in county boundaries been made.

Baldwin vs. Wickman, 3 Wyo. 208.   [R. S. 1887, Sec. 3978.]

STATE TREASURER AUTHORIZED TO RECEIVE DONATIONS FOR SCHOOLS.

Sec. 622. Whenever the state of Wyoming shall be entitled to receive any moneys or funds from the United States of America, or from
any other source or authority, to be expended for the benefit of the public
schools of the state, or held or in any manner applied for their benefit,
the state treasurer is hereby authorized to receive and receipt for such
moneys or funds, and to make such application and use of the same as
may be required by law. Should such moneys or funds be donated to the
state, and should the act of donation require such moneys or funds to be
applied or held, or used in a particular manner, they shall be so applied.

[R. S. 1887, Sec. 3981.]

LIABILITY OF TREASURER FOR SCHOOL MONEY.

Sec. 623. The state treasurer shall faithfully account for all moneys
or funds received pursuant to the foregoing section, and he and his sureties upon his official bond shall be liable for any failure to so account for
such moneys or funds.

[R. S. 1887, Sec. 3982.]

SCHOOL BOARD MAY ESTABLISH MANUAL TRAINING SCHOOLS.

Sec. 624. The school board of any district in the state shall have
power to establish and locate industrial and manual training schools, in
connection with the public schools of said district.

[S. L. 1895, Ch. 88.]

LAND INCOME FUNDS AVAILABLE—WHEN.

Sec. 625. On the fifteenth day of January, eighteen hundred and
ninety-nine, and on the fifteenth day of January of each second year thereafter, any and all moneys which shall be in either of the following land
income funds shall become available, and may be used for the following
purposes, respectively:

First—The "Deaf, Dumb and Blind Land Income Fund," for the support, maintenance and education of all such deaf, dumb and blind persons as are or may hereafter become charges upon the state.

Second—The "Insane Asylum Land Income Fund," for the support
and maintenance of the state insane asylum and the inmates thereof.

Third—The "Fish Hatchery Land Income Fund," for the support and
maintenance of the state fish hatchery in Albany county.

Fourth—The "Penitentiary in Albany County Land Income Fund,"
for the support and maintenance of the penitentiary located in Albany
county, and the care and subsistence of the convicts therein.

Fifth—The "University Land Income Fund," for the support and
maintenance of the state university at Laramie, the same to be paid by
the state treasurer to the treasurer of the board of trustees of the state
university upon the warrant of the state auditor to be issued upon request
of said board of trustees.

Sixth—The "State, Charitable, Educational, Penal and Reformatory
Institutions Land Income Fund," for the custody, support and mainten-

37

ance of state convicts and persons confined at the expense of the state in reformatory institutions within or without the state.

Seventh—The "Penal, Reformatory or Educational Institution in Carbon County Land Income Fund," for and toward the completion, furnishing and maintenance of the penitentiary at Rawlins, in Carbon county.

Eighth—The "Miners' Hospital Land Income Fund," for the support and maintenance of the Wyoming General Hospital, at Rock Springs.

Ninth—The "Public Buildings at the Capital Land Income Fund," for the care, repair, maintenance and furnishing of the capitol building.

Tenth—The "Poor Farm in Fremont County Land Income Fund," for the care, repair, maintenance and improvement of the poor farm in Fremont County.

On the fifteenth day of January, nineteen hundred and one, and on the fifteenth day of January of each second year thereafter, it shall be the duty of the state treasurer to make a report to the governor and to the senate and house of representatives, showing the amount of money in each of the said land income funds on that date.

[S. L. 1897, Ch. 30.]

TEACHERS' CERTIFICATES.

Sec. 626. There are hereby established four grades of teachers' certificates; one to be known as a state or professional certificate, and county certificates of the first, second and third grades, which certificates shall show the branches in which the holder has been examined, and his or her relative attainments in each branch. No person shall receive a certificate who is known to the examining officer, or board, to be of immoral character, who is deficient in learning or ability to teach, or who does not write and speak the English language with facility and correctness.

[S. L. 1899, Ch. 70, Sec. 1.]

SUBJECTS OF EXAMINATION.

Sec. 627. Every applicant for a certificate shall be examined in the subjects hereinafter mentioned, for the several grades, respectively, as follows: For the third grade, in orthoepy, orthography, reading, penmanship, arithmetic, language lessons, English grammar, geography, civil government, the history and constitution of the United States, the constitution of the state of Wyoming, physiology and hygiene, and the theory and practice of teaching. If the applicants shall pass an examination in these branches with an average of seventy per cent., they shall receive a third grade certificate. If the markings of said applicant shall average of eighty-five per cent., a second grade certificate shall be issued. For the first grade certificate, the applicant shall pass an examination in all of the foregoing branches required in examination for second and third grade certificates, and also in rhetoric, elementary algebra, natural philosophy, plane geometry, English literature, political economy, physical geography and bookkeeping.

[S. L. 1899, Ch. 70, Sec. 2.]

TIME CERTIFICATE IS GOOD.

Sec. 628. The third grade certificate shall entitle the holder to teach for the period of one year; and a third grade certificate shall not be issued to any teacher more than once; the second grade certificate shall entitle the holder to teach for one year; the first grade certificate shall entitle the holder to teach for a period of two years; and the state or professional certificate shall entitle the holder to teach in the graded and high schools of the state for a period of five years, at the end of which time, if the teacher has been actively engaged for two years prior thereto in educational work, the state superintendent, or the state board of examiners and the state superintendent, may endorse said certificate, and this endorsement shall entitle the holder to teach for another period of five years.

[S. L. 1899, Ch. 70, Sec. 2.]

EXAMINING BOARD.

Sec. 629. There shall be established in the state of Wyoming a state board of examiners, which shall be composed of three members to be selected and appointed by the superintendent of public instruction from the principals of high schools and city superintendents of schools in the state and the faculty of the state university. This board shall serve without compensation other than actual expenses and transportation. It shall be the duty of said board to meet at some convenient place and prepare, for the use of the county superintendents of the various counties, uniform examination questions, and they may prescribe rules and regulations for the taking of such examinations. They shall have the power to hold examinations, and on their recommendation, the superintendent of public instruction shall issue professional certificates as provided in this article.

[S. L. 1899, Ch. 70, Sec. 3.]

APPLICANTS FOR PROFESSIONAL CERTIFICATES.

Sec. 630. Applicants for professional certificates shall show themselves to be competent to teach all the branches required for the issuing of a first grade certificate in the counties, and, in addition thereto, shall show that they are qualified to teach all of the branches usually taught in the high schools and academic courses.

[S. L. 1899, Ch. 70, Sec. 4.]

EXAMINATIONS BY COUNTY SUPERINTENDENTS.

Sec. 631. County superintendents shall hold regular examinations in their counties at least twice in each year, and one of such examinations shall be held at the close of the teachers' institute held in their respective counties; the county superintendent may require all teachers to pass a written examination prepared by the state board of examiners, and, where such examination is in writing, shall mark and file said written examination papers in his office, there to be kept for the period of one year where it may be seen by any school board desiring to examine the same. Provided, that where a teacher has had professional training in some reputable normal training school for teachers, has taught successfully, and presents a diploma or other sufficient evidence of his or her qualifications to teach, the county superintendent may issue a certificate to such person stating the facts and setting forth the qualifications of such teacher. And provided further, that all persons who are graduates of the University of Wyoming, and upon whom have been conferred the degree of Bachelor of Arts; or the degree of Bachelor of Science; or the degree of Bachelor of Pedagogy, or Didactics; shall be exempt from taking the teachers' examination for certificates of the first, second and third grades, as provided in this article, and upon the presentation of their diploma granted by the University of Wyoming to the county superintendent of schools. it shall be the duty of such county superintendents to issue to such person a first grade certificate.

[S. L. 1899, Ch. 70, Sec. 5.]

INVESTMENT OF LAND FUNDS.

Sec. 88. All permanent funds arising from the sale of state lands and any permanent addition thereto may, and whenever practicable shall be invested by the treasurer of the state, with the approval of the governor and attorney general, in bonds of the United States or of the state of Wyoming, or in bonds issued by school districts within this state, or registered county bonds of the state, or interest bearing warrants of this state. The interest only shall be used for the purpose for which the grant of lands was made.

[S. L. 1895, Ch. 67, Sec. 1.]

www.ingramcontent.com/pod-product-compliance
Lightning Source LLC
Chambersburg PA
CBHW021603270326
41931CB00009B/1355